CORE WRITING SKILLS

How to

Use Technology to Write and Publish

Sara Howell

PowerKiDS press™

New York

Published in 2014 by The Rosen Publishing Group, Inc.
29 East 21st Street, New York, NY 10010

First Edition

Editor: Amelie von Zumbusch
Book Design: Andrew Povolny
Photo Research: Katie Stryker

Photo Credits: Cover Blend Images/Thinkstock: p. 5 Tara Moore/Taxi/Getty Images; p. 6 Yellow Dog Productions/Digital Visions/Getty Images; p. 7 Katrina Wittkamp/Digital Vision/Getty Images; p. 8 LWA/ Jay Newman/Blend Images/Getty Images; p. 9 Andrew Lundquist/Shutterstock.com; p.10 SilviaJansen/ E+/Getty Images; p. 12 xavier gallego morell/Shutterstock.com; p. 14 Mark Bowden/E+/Getty Images; p. 16 Darren Baker/Shutterstock.com; p. 17 Pressmaster/Shutterstock.com; p. 19 Jan Kranendonk/ Shutterstock.com; p. 21 Diane Diederich/E+/Getty Images; p. 22 Peathegee Inc./Blend Images/ Getty Images.

Library of Congress Cataloging-in-Publication Data

Howell, Sara.
 How to use technology to write and publish / By Sara Howell. — First Edition.
     pages cm. — (Core writing skills)
 Includes index.
 ISBN 978-1-4777-2911-3 (library) — ISBN 978-1-4777-3000-3 (pbk.) —
 ISBN 978-1-4777-3070-6 (6-pack)
 1. Word processing—Juvenile literature. 2. Electronic publishing—Juvenile literature.
 3. Web publishing—Juvenile literature. 4. Word processing in education. I. Title.
 Z52.4.H59 2014
 005.52—dc23
                                    2013026332

Manufactured in the United States of America

CPSIA Compliance Information: Batch #W14PK4: For Further Information contact Rosen Publishing, New York, New York at 1-800-237-9932

CONTENTS

DISCOVER TECHNOLOGY

Have you used a computer or sent a text message today? Have you ever used the Internet to write a report for school? Computers, cell phones, and the Internet are all forms of technology.

Technology has changed the way we get and share information. In the past, students had to read through many books to find information on a **topic**. They wrote pieces either by hand or with a typewriter. Sharing a piece of writing meant making copies and handing them out. Today, all of that can be done with a few clicks of a mouse!

Writing Tip

About 75 percent of US homes have a computer. If you do not have a computer at home, use one at school or your local library.

Technology has not only made it easier to write pieces, but also made it easier to share what you have written with others.

DIGITAL LITERACY

To take full advantage of new technologies, you will need to learn a new set of skills. These skills are often called **digital literacy**. Literacy is the ability to read and write. Digital literacy involves finding, sorting, and creating information on computers.

Some schools have classes, computer labs, and more to help students gain digital literacy. Do you ever use a computer or tablet at school?

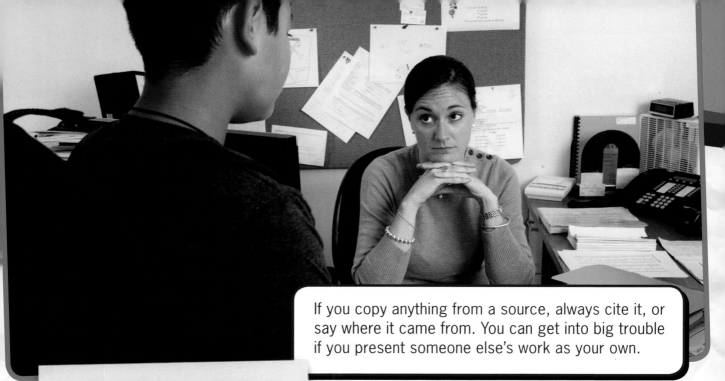

If you copy anything from a source, always cite it, or say where it came from. You can get into big trouble if you present someone else's work as your own.

Writing Tip

Copying another person's work is called plagiarism. Be sure you cite all sources and put information into your own words.

An important part of digital literacy is thinking **critically** about the information that you find. You will need to decide if information is useful to your project and whether it comes from a source that is **credible**, or truthful. You should also know how to **cite** a website where you find information.

READY FOR RESEARCH

The first step in digital literacy is knowing where to look for information on a topic. If you are using the Internet, a **search engine** is a great place to start. Begin by searching for key words and ideas. If you are looking for information about zebras, you might type "zebra diet" or "zebra habitat" into the search engine.

A few extra words can make a search more successful. "Mustang" will turn up sites about both horses and cars, while "mustang horse" will focus more on animals.

Did you know that the US National Park Service has a website for each national park? This kid is visiting Glacier National Park, in Montana.

Writing Tip

Encyclopedias have information on many different topics. Many encyclopedias have online versions that you can use.

You will likely find lots of information on the Internet. Not all information comes from credible sources, though. Websites run by zoos, museums, and the US government are good places to find information that is true and up-to-date.

TAKING NOTES

As you read through websites, remember to take notes. You can even use a computer or tablet! Start by opening a blank **document** on your screen. When you find a useful fact on the Internet, click over to the document. Type a few key words that will help you remember the fact. You can also bookmark any websites that you may want to come back to later.

You can also take notes by hand. However, notes taken on a computer are easier to reorganize later on.

Notes on Sea Otters

More than one million hairs per square inch
http://www.montereybayaquarium.org/efc/otter.aspx

Live in Pacific Ocean
Use tools
http://www.sheddaquarium.org/seaotters.html

Eat 25% of their weight in food every day
http://www.defenders.org/sea-otter/basic-facts

When you have the information you need, **organize** it and plan your piece. You can cut and paste your notes so related information is grouped together. Then open up a new document and start writing!

Writing Tip

Different sources may give you different information. Find at least two sources that agree to be sure your facts are true.

DRAW IT OUT

Your piece of writing should convey ideas and information as clearly as possible. You might find that some information is easier to understand when it is shown as a **graphic organizer**, photo, or illustration. For example, if you are writing about population growth in your state, you could use a graph to show changes over time. If you describe the features of a platypus, a photo can help readers visualize the animal.

This girl is taking a photograph of some mushrooms. You can upload photographs from digital cameras and smartphones to use them in your piece of writing.

You can create your own graphic organizers and illustrations on a computer using drawing programs and online **templates**. You can then paste these illustrations right into your writing document.

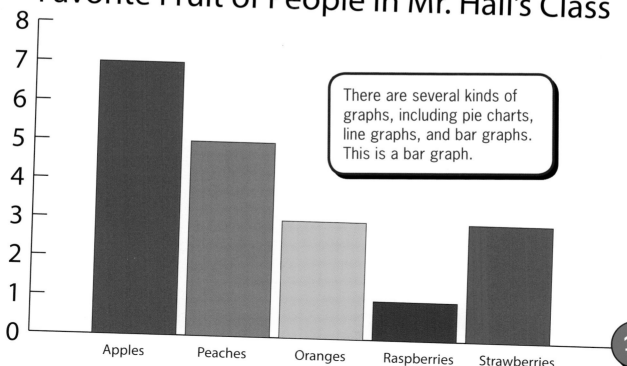

Favorite Fruit of People in Mr. Hall's Class

There are several kinds of graphs, including pie charts, line graphs, and bar graphs. This is a bar graph.

Apples   Peaches   Oranges   Raspberries   Strawberries

FIXING UP

When you have written your piece, check it for any mistakes in spelling or **grammar**. Finding and fixing these mistakes is called editing. Many computer programs will underline or highlight spelling mistakes and sentences that do not use proper punctuation.

Read over your piece and look for any spelling or grammar errors that the computer program missed. Computer programs will not catch every error!

Jackie Robinson was a great baseball player. He was the first African American to play major leage baseball. He played for the Brooklyn Dogers. he is my hero.

Computer programs often underline mistakes. Here, spelling mistakes are underlined in red, while grammar mistakes are underlined in green.

You should also reread your piece as if you were seeing it for the first time. Does it flow, or move well from one idea to the next? Do not be afraid to **revise**, or change, any parts that do not make sense. Using technology to edit and revise keeps you from having to rewrite your entire piece by hand!

Writing Tip

Edit and revise with a computer's cut-and-paste feature. Select a paragraph, cut it, and then paste it where you want it to be.

MAKING CONNECTIONS

Have you ever worked on a group writing project? In a group project, everyone does a certain job. Technology can be very useful for researching and writing as a group. Group members can use email to share their work with each other. They can also use video chat to talk over ideas and ask questions.

You can use a smartphone, computer, or tablet to read a piece that someone has sent to you for feedback.

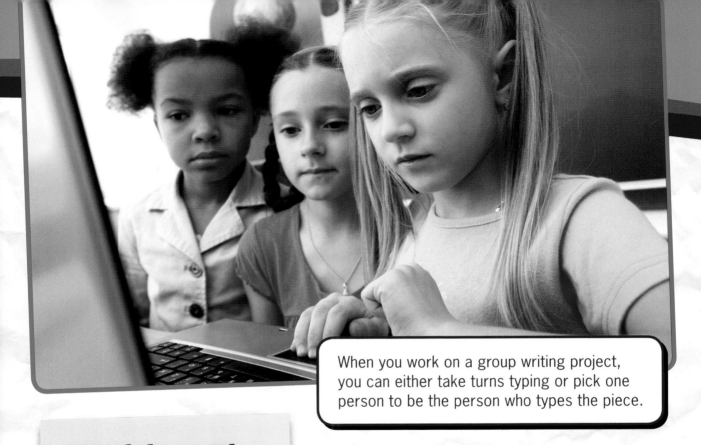

When you work on a group writing project, you can either take turns typing or pick one person to be the person who types the piece.

Writing Tip

When you give someone feedback, be specific. If you like or dislike something, be sure to explain why.

Technology can also help you get **feedback** on your writing from others. Feedback can include notes, edits, and suggestions on how to make your piece better. See if your teacher will set up a website where students can give each other feedback on their work.

SPREAD THE WORD!

Some people write simply for themselves. Most writers, though, write with the hope that others will read their work. When someone prints a piece of writing so that other people can read it, it is called publishing.

There are publishing companies around the world that print the work of professional writers. You do not need to be a professional to share your writing with others, though. Computers make it quick and easy to print pieces of writing. You and your friends might enjoy working together to write and print out a book of short stories or poems!

Writing Tip

Desktop publishing software can help you create a cover and page layout, or design, for any writing that you would like to publish.

If you decide to put together your own book, remember to make a cover for it.

DIGITAL PUBLISHING

In the past, publishing meant printing a piece of writing on paper to share. Today, it means something else, too. Writing can be published on the Internet and shared with the world in seconds!

There are many websites where you may be able to share your writing. See if your school has a website that publishes student work. You can also search the Internet for writing contests for kids. With a parent's permission, you could even start your own blog. You can continue to post new writing on your blog and get feedback from people around the world.

Writing Tip

Always be careful not to put any personal information on the Internet. Get a parent's permission before signing up for any websites or contests.

When you publish your work online, it is easy to share with friends and relatives who live around the world.

PUBLISHING PASSION

When we think of published writing, we often think of stories and poems. You can write and publish any type of writing that interests you, though. Try starting a family newsletter and emailing it to family members who live far away.

If you have an idea for how to make your community a better place, email a local politician. If you love koalas, create a book about them for a younger sibling. Today's technology makes it faster and easier to write and share work than ever before!

If you could write about any topic in the world, what would you pick?

GLOSSARY

cite (SYT) To call attention to or give credit to a source.

credible (KREH-duh-bel) Believable and trustworthy.

critically (KRIH-tih-kuh-lee) With careful judgment.

digital literacy (DIH-juh-tul LIH-tuh-ruh-see) The ability to use computers, the Internet, and other technology well.

document (DOK-yoo-ment) A piece of text stored on a computer.

feedback (FEED-bak) Suggestions from people who have reviewed something.

grammar (GRA-mer) The rules of how words combine to form sentences.

graphic organizer (GRA-fik OR-guh-ny-zer) A chart, graph, or picture that sorts facts and ideas and makes them clear.

organize (OR-guh-nyz) To have things neat and in order.

revise (rih-VYZ) To make changes to or improvements in something.

search engine (SERCH EN-jin) A computer program that searches the Internet for websites.

templates (TEM-pluts) Formats into which information can be filled so that documents or files do not need to be created from scratch.

topic (TAH-pik) The subject of a piece of writing.

INDEX

WEBSITES

Due to the changing nature of Internet links, PowerKids Press has developed an online list of websites related to the subject of this book. This site is updated regularly. Please use this link to access the list:

www.powerkidslinks.com/cws/tech/